SEO

Search Engine Optimization

QUICKLY LEARN HOW TO DOMINATE THE SEARCH ENGINES AND WHAT YOU NEED TO KNOW ABOUT THE GOOGLE PANDA AND PENGUIN

Amanda Eliza Bertha

SEO: Search Engine Optimization - Quickly Learn How to Dominate the Search Engines and What You Need to Know About the Google Panda and Penguin

SEO: Search Engine Optimization

By

Amanda Eliza Bertha

SEO: Search Engine Optimization

Copyright © 2012 by Amanda Eliza Bertha

Disclaimers

This book is presented to you for informational purposes only and is not a substitution for any professional advice. The contents herein are based on the views and opinions of the author and all associated contributors.

While every effort has been made by the author and all associated contributors to present accurate and up to date information within this document, it is apparent technologies rapidly change. Therefore, the author and all associated contributors reserve the right to update the contents and information provided herein as these changes progress. The author and/or all associated contributors take no responsibility for any errors or omissions if such discrepancies exist within this document.

The author and all other contributors accept no responsibility for any consequential actions taken, whether monetary, legal, or otherwise, by any and all readers of the materials provided. It is the reader's sole responsibility to seek professional advice before taking any action on their part.

Readers results will vary based on their skill level and individual perception of the contents herein, and thus no guarantees, monetarily or otherwise, can be made accurately. Therefore, no guarantees are made.

Amanda's Other Books

Economic Crisis: World Food System - The Battle against Poverty, Pollution and Corruption

Flood Your Websites and Blogs with Free Traffic: Quickly Learn How to Send Visitors to Your Web Sites the Organic Way

Quickly Dominate Social Media Marketing: The Ultimate Guide Top Tips to Pinterest, Google+, Facebook, Twitter, Instagram, LinkedIn and YouTube Viral Marketing

Anti-Aging Guide Top Tips: Inspiration and Helpful
Advice to Help You Feel Gorgeous and Look Younger

Home Quick Makeovers Top Tips: Learn How to Design,
Decorate and Furnish Your Ideal Home

SEO: Search Engine Optimization

Table of Contents

SEO: Search Engine Optimization

Introduction

Rather than go into a long explanation, here is a brief bit of background to the introduction of the World Wide Web to the general population. The reason for this is that without understanding how the internet developed, it is difficult to grasp the situation where seeking page one of Google means so much to the web business world.

To begin at the beginning we have to go back to 1980 when Tim Berners-Lee came up with the concept of hypertext as a way to share information. It was hard for scientists to share ideas across the country because they were limited to text and much of their exploration involved drawings and sketches. Eventually, Berners-Lee realized that the power of sharing information would increase immensely if he could find a way to share the information using the protocols that had become available for sharing communications.

Actually, the internet concept had been in use since the Bay of Pigs invasion in 1961 when the American government realized that having all their command information in one location was very dangerous. A single hit could wipe out communications and cripple the country.

Here is a tiny bit of background on the Bay of Pigs Invasion. It was an April 1961 invasion of Cuba carried out by Brigade 2506. This Brigade was a militia group that the CIA paid for and trained. The plan was for the Brigade to overthrow the Cuban government ruled by Osvaldo Dorticós Torrado. However, the CIA-trained Brigade 2506 was defeated by a Cuban army led by Cuba's Prime

Minister Fidel Castro. This defeat was a shock to the American government and focused attention on the need to protect the country in the Cold War that had been underway for several years.

With the possibility of more defeat, with communist Cuba hovering so close to the country, there was an acute awareness of a serious problem. What if the communication system was destroyed completely? And it could be because there was one central core to the communications. Brilliant scientists at the top universities studied the problem. Leonard Kleinrock, a graduate student at MIT, had discovered something called packet switching and in 1961, he wrote a paper about it.

Very simply stated, packet switching means that messages are divided up into packets that are sent in little pieces and when the packets all arrive at their destination, they are reunited. This was the heart of the solution to centralized communications. The US government's defense research department set up the ARPAnet (Advanced Research Projects Agency

Network) which was built on using packet switching. ARPAnet was the grandfather of the Internet as we know it.

Because ARPAnet connected universities and research centers, it became a way for researchers to share their information and this is why Berners-Lee was looking for a faster and more comprehensive way to share information over the network. His search for a way to share information led to the development of hypertext markup language (HTML) and then a browser that allowed people to see the graphics and details of the research carried out at other institutions. His first browser was the NeXTStep WorldWideWeb application which he created in 1990. On August 6, 1991, Berners-Lee presented the first web page ever to the world. It was the CERN (European Organization for Nuclear Research) site.

However this book is about search engine optimization and it is time to move to the web as we know it today and how search engines came to be so powerful and why Google keeps changing its algorithms.

The World Wide Web Emerges

The power of html and this method of sharing information exploded on the academic community and spread out to the general population. NeXTStep WorldWideWeb was renamed Nexus and Berners-Lee released the source code into the public domain in 1993. You could edit the hypertext and view it with Nexus. The next browsers developed only allowed people to view the hypertext.

People began to build their own websites. MTV had one of the first websites, appearing in 1993. By the end of 1994, there were about ten thousand websites in the entire world. In 1995, a new website emerged and that was Jerry's Guide to the World Wide Web. Later it changed its name to Yahoo and then to Yahoo!

Yahoo! was the creation of Jerry Yang and David Filo, graduate students in electrical engineering at Stanford. They came up with the idea in January

1994, It was incorporated on March 1, 1995. As the number of website grew so quickly, Yang and Filo came up with the idea of creating a directory and registered the domain name yahoo.com on January 18, 1995.

In case you are wondering about the name, Yahoo stands for Yet Another Hierarchical Officious Oracle. However, yahoo was a common epithet for rural people from the South and Filo was from the southern USA.

The problem began right about this time as the number of web pages grew, it was becoming harder and harder to find what you wanted online. There was more and more information and it was becoming a real challenge to find your way through the mass of pages. Yahoo! was just what people needed to help them find their way through the web.

Google Begins

In 1995 Sergey Brin and Larry Page met. Page had just graduated from the University of Michigan and Brin was showing him around Stanford. When Page did decide to enter Stanford, he and Brin collaborated on a search engine. They were both computer science graduate students and the World Wide Web was in full flight. They called their project BackRub at first. Then they decided it needed a better name so chose Googol. Googol refers to a very large number – 1 with 100 zeroes. A million has nine zeroes so you can imagine how large this number is.

The two men were only in their early twenties at the time and you can see the playful nature of their naming conventions, just as with Yahoo! This may have been serious stuff but these were students playing with an idea. They planned to systematize all the information on the World Wide Web. The domain googol.com was already taken and rather than deal with the problem of trying to obtain that name, the men chose to register google.com. In September 1998, Page and Brin opened their Google office in Menlo Park in a garage. Within months, the superior algorithm of Google showed its impact on the search engine world. By the end of 2001, Google had three billion documents in its index.

SEO Explained

This has been a longish explanation of search engines but in order to understand search engine optimization or SEO, it helps to understand the rapid growth of the World Wide Web and the need for people to find ways to have their websites land at the top page of search engines, in particular Google.

Google ruled the Ethernet waves. On one side of the search engine world there were (and are) people like Berners-Lee, Yang, Filo, Page, Brin and a whole legion of similar technical minds whose goal was to make sharing information relevant and accessible.

On the other side of the World Wide Web universe, there were (and are) the entrepreneurs and marketers and web gurus whose goals include being easily found online. If they could discover the perfect way to optimize their websites for search engine optimization, they could be at the top of the list of websites that any search engine found for web surfers.

SEO – The Early Years

In the early years of search engines, there were also early years of SEO. Think of the growth of search engines and the growth of ways to attract search engines as a kind of dance. On one hand, brilliant minds are trying to find a way to evaluate and reveal the good web pages that are appearing in increasing numbers on the web. On the other hand, the people putting up the growing numbers of web sites are trying to figure out how to make their web pages appear at the top of the directory lists.

Since the whole concept is very new and constantly changing, the algorithms are also changing, being refined so that they are more accurate. There is no pattern that is set in stone for measuring the value of the pages. By 1996, web masters were figuring out that keywords were important. Remember, at this time, Google was still Backrub and a work in progress. In those days, websites were submitted to Yahoo in the hopes of being indexed by that paramount search engine.

Just a side note, there were other search engines in the very early days such as Wandex, a 1993 entry into the search engine world. It involved a web crawled known as World Wide Web Wanderer. It disappeared over time but another 1993 earch engine, Aliweb, and the 1994 Lycos are still in use. Yahoo offered more and it was the place to be recognized so energetic web masters spammed Yahoo with submissions in the early days. The notion was that the more submissions of s particular site, the more important the big search engine might think it was. For the last years of the 1990s, this was about all there was to SEO.

PageRank

Google was in the game and by the turn of the century it was becoming the king of algorithm logic for websites. One of the ways it measured successful entrants in the website competitions was with PageRank (PR). This is still a major measurement for websites. PR7 sites are the cream of the crop. A lot of people think that this refers to the ranking of a web page.

It doesn't. PageRank got its name from Larry Page. Google revamped the entire way that websites were ranked with astounding new algorithms. PageRank is a Google trademark and a patented process with Stanford University owning the patent. Google bought the exclusive license rights to the patent. Google gave Stanford 1.8 million shares for the use of these rights.

Page and Brin developed PageRank in 1996 and was based on the concept that link popularity was the best way to measure a website's value. This was back when the men were researching search engines and before they formalized Google. PageRank is at the heart of Google's search engine power.

PageRank is essentially a probability distribution that assesses the probability that someone will randomly reach a particular website. PageRank measures the likelihood by making computations based on iterations of searches. The higher the PageRank, the greater the likelihood that people will find the website.

Early SEO efforts involved using lists of words that were guaranteed to attract the attention of the web crawlers that fed the algorithms. One of the methods that worked for a while was stuffing the meta data with keywords. Other tricks involved using keywords that search engines could see but people could not. There were even sites that included text written in the same color as the background so that the words were there but unseen by website visitors.

A particular method that some people used was to include words such as "sex" which was a highly sought after word. The websites often had nothing to do with sex at all but the web masters believed that if they could get traffic to their websites, people would stay. It was not exactly fair to trick people into landing on a site and soon the big search engine cracked down on keyword stuffing.

SEO Advice and What Works

This section covers the cutting edge advice for SEO in the first few years of this century. It was accepted and agreed that SEO was the be all and end all when it came to getting traffic to your website. The only real concern that many website owners had was how to get the most traffic for the least cost. Since some of these methods have lost their power, the information in this section are really a bit of a history lesson and not a guide on how to optimize your websites today.

Link Exchanges

Getting more links into your website was considered a great way to make it look appealing to the search engines which in turn made it look like a great place to visit. After all, a whole lot of other websites liked it well enough to link to it.

Does this still work?

Yes, if the links are real. That is, these are links that other website owners sought out from you and not links that you purchased from link farms. You can network to get in touch with other pertinent websites to see if they are interested in being associated with you.

What went wrong?

As Google's algorithms became more astute, they were able to discern which links were authentic links and which ones came from sites that were artificially creating and delivering links. Well, to be accurate, the links were real but they were not high quality. The web sites existed only to provide links so that websites would look like they had hundreds of quality links.

Keyword Laden Articles

When the need to provide content became important, the chosen method was to have articles on the website. Five or ten articles rich in keywords gave the illusion of value to the site. Writing fast enough to fill up websites was a challenge for many website owners.

Does this still work?

Content is the key to having a great website that Google loves. Good fresh content that is accurate, informative, and current will bring people to visit and return. Using the keyword in the title and first and last paragraph is ideal for good SEO. The emphasis should be on the quality of the writing and the focus on the subject.

What went wrong?

To meet the demand for good web copy, the solution was to use articles from directories or spin articles or outsource the writing.

The problem with directory articles is that over time, these were recognized as duplicate content which took away the value of them as something that would make people come to your website for advice. People who are searching for a topic run a good chance of finding the same content on different websites.

Spun articles are often poor quality. And poor quality is not a way to get people coming back to your site. If you are selling information on your website and your articles are poorly spun, how much confidence is the reader going to have in your offering?

People frequently outsource the writing of their articles and ask for a specific density of keywords. However, sometimes this is not properly rendered and the articles have an unnatural feel to them.

One of the worst mistakes to make is to have a great title and a good lead-in sentence and nothing else. If you go to a website looking for information on a specific topic and you read the title, Seven Great

Ways to Lose Weight (for instance) and the first line is "Here are seven great ways to lose weight" you are pleased. But then you read the rest of the articles and aside from having seven points, there is nothing there about losing weight, it is likely that you will never return to that site and for sure you will not sign up for anything that it has to offer.

As for outsourcing, it can be expensive so a lot of web owners try to get a deal and do not pay attention to the quality of the writing.

Example:

This is from an outsourced article on erectile dysfunction. Imagine you are seeking real advice on this issue and you read an article that includes this paragraph:

But before you will use erectile dysfunction cures, it is important that you will seek for medical consultation so that you can get solution from the problem easily. The good thing about prior consultation is that you will also be given with additional non-medication related treatments that can also restore your normal erectile dysfunction problems.

Huh? What does this mean? As a reader, do you really want to waste your time trying to figure out what this nonsense means?

Google changed the algorithm to deal with the immense amount of garbage that was appearing online. Google's mandate is to offer web surfers an easy way to find what they are looking for. When the results are pages and pages of trashy, non-informative, poorly spun crap, Google had to step up and find ways to get through the mass of bad articles.

How to benefit safely?

Have real quality. Write the articles yourself or hire a good writer.

Google Response to Low Quality

Google's algorithm changes are not something new, as you have seen so far in this book. They are an ongoing effort to keep the search engine relevant for its purpose which is to help people find the information that they want to find. The more threats to this goal, the more diligently Google works to find ways to overcome the threats.

This does not mean that Google is specifically out to get web owners who try to "game" the system. However, in gaming the system with artificial SEO efforts, the end result is usually poor quality websites with the single intention of tricking people into believing the site has authority and valid offerings as shown on Google through PageRank and position. Here are some of the algorithm changes that have taken place in recent years.

Google Caffeine Algorithm

Caffeine began in August 2009 and put in place in June, 2010. It was a change in Google's architecture which was designed to speed up searches and handle the fast-changing information that comes from places such as Facebook and Twitter. Keywords were given more weight in ranking as was the domain's age. This, like many of the updates in algorithms was merely designed to respond to the changes in how information was being released on the internet.

Panda Algorithm Update

The Panda update was specifically aimed at so-called thin sites. These are the junkie kind of sites that were SEOed with artificial SEO methods. The change was obvious as news and social networking websites jumped higher in the search engine while sites with mostly advertising plummeted. There were concerns that Google was not able to handle the huge influx of scraper sites and the Panda update was a concerted effort to content with these sites.

The name is not a made up name or an acronym. It came from the engineer who was behind the major new algorithmic change, Navneet Panda.

The effect was dramatic when Panda was rolled out in February 2011 and each time it was tweaked and updated, the ripples continued to be felt in the internet marketing world.

Google blogged about the requirements for a high-quality site, offering the following 23 points (the blog is available at http://googlewebmastercentral.blogspot.com/2011/05/more-guidance-on-building-high-quality.html):

- Would you trust the information presented in this article?
- Is this article written by an expert or enthusiast who knows the topic well, or is it more shallow in nature?
- Does the site have duplicate, overlapping, or redundant articles on the same or similar topics with slightly different keyword variations?
- Would you be comfortable giving your credit card information to this site?

- Does this article have spelling, stylistic, or factual errors?
- Are the topics driven by genuine interests of readers of the site, or does the site generate content by attempting to guess what might rank well in search engines?
- Does the article provide original content or information, original reporting, original research, or original analysis?
- Does the page provide substantial value when compared to other pages in search results?
- How much quality control is done on content?
- Does the article describe both sides of a story?
- Is the site a recognized authority on its topic?
- Is the content mass-produced by or outsourced to a large number of creators, or spread across a large network of sites, so that individual pages or sites don't get as much attention or care?
- Was the article edited well, or does it appear sloppy or hastily produced?
- For a health related query, would you trust information from this site?
- Would you recognize this site as an authoritative source when mentioned by name?

- Does this article provide a complete or comprehensive description of the topic?
- Does this article contain insightful analysis or interesting information that is beyond obvious?
- Is this the sort of page you'd want to bookmark, share with a friend, or recommend?
- Does this article have an excessive amount of ads that distract from or interfere with the main content?
- Would you expect to see this article in a printed magazine, encyclopedia or book?
- Are the articles short, unsubstantial, or otherwise lacking in helpful specifics?
- Are the pages produced with great care and attention to detail vs. less attention to detail?
- Would users complain when they see pages from this site?

The entire list of points is reprinted here because this is the essence of what you need to consider in order to have your website thrive online.

Google's Panda used artificial intelligence fed by data from real people who quality tested websites. The changes have been real game-changers for

Google search engine optimization techniques. One of the big changes is that PageRank which was there before Google was reduced in its importance in the world of Google search engines. PageRank is important in its own way but once website gurus learned how to trick Google into accepting lower quality websites as high quality entities, it lost a lot of its value. When Panda found pages that were substandard according to its algorithm, it penalized not just the page but the entire website.

Google still runs Panda from time to time to catch the thin sites. By September 2012, Panda was finding fewer and fewer offending pages.

Penguin Algorithm Update

As part of the ongoing process of keeping Google relevant, in April 2012, Google released its Penguin update. This had an impact on more than three percent of English language search queries. Penguin took direct aim at websites that use black-hat methods for SEO. These include some of the approaches discussed earlier in this book such as link schemes, duplicate content, and keyword stuffing. To state it simply, people who tried to game the search engines were hit hard.

This is a big change from previous algorithm changes which were aimed at best rankings methods and Panda which was aimed at finding a way to demote websites with poor content. Penguin was hitting right at the core of one of the problems which was the use of black-hat SEO.

Just before Penguin, in January 2012, there was a page layout algorithm. It was looking for websites that did not have a lot of content in the area known as above the fold. This refers to the top half of a newspaper, above the place where the papers are folded. This is considered the prime placement in a newspaper. This is the part that is visible when newspapers are sold in boxes or at newsstands. In terms of a website, this is the part of the website that appears on your screen when you load the site into your browser.

What This Means to the Internet Marketer

Panda and Penguin seem to be poised to stay and other changes are taking place. Here is an example, and if you have studied internet marketing, you may have heard of the power of this technique – exact match domains.

There were courses taught on selling digital products and tangible products using exact match domains. This was the golden secret to achieving a high ranking. Get on page one of Google guaranteed with exact match domain names. This was the battle cry of many people selling advice on how to make it to the top.

If you were selling sewing machines, you didn't want to settle for sewingmachines.com. It was better if you got a domain that had the brand and model name. Singerxx34.com (if Singer had a model xx34) was a better choice. Thousands upon thousands of exact match domains were registered and people worked hard at creating meaningful sites.

Then came the EMD (exact match domain) update. Matt Cutts, known as Google's head of webspam, tweeted it just like this:

> Minor weather report: small upcoming Google algo change will reduce low-quality "exact match" domains in search results.

That was at 4:43 pm on September 28, 2012.

The hunt is ongoing and most of what we learned over the past 10 years is no longer valid when it comes to getting highly ranked in Google.

People who were raking it in with their websites suddenly had a rude awakening. Their sites that they had spent thousands raising up in the ranks were suddenly de-indexed. Their websites are gone from Google and no one is able to find them using the good old search engine.

It was a career ender for many in the dedicated world of website marketing. People who were selling tangible products through their exact match domain websites because they were highly ranked for that particular key word saw sales plummet.

The huge legions of SEO writers who were kept busy writing for web owners are finding a change in their work loads too. Fewer web owners are looking for SEO writing because they are confused about the future. The whole game has changed and no one is quite sure what to do.

The big question is:

Is SEO Dead?

The answer may sound confusing but it is both "yes" and "no." SEO as you may know it is dead. If you have a hard drive full of reports on SEO that you carefully collected over the years, you might as well dump them. Google's changes are responding to all the techniques that are the body of those reports. Google knows about the backlinks you can buy on Fiverr or in some of the forums. Google knows about the inaccurate and lightweight articles you can buy for pennies and spin for nothing. They won't let these efforts create a place for you anywhere near the top of Google.

That is the "yes SEO is dead" response.

However, as long as there are search engines, the better tuned a web page is to the search engine's purpose, the better the page will rank – regardless of the algorithm in place. So looking at SEO from this perspective, the response is "No. SEO is not dead."

The rest of this book will look at the best ways to deal with SEO in a positive and productive manner.

SEO after Panda and Penguin

What can you do moving forward with a new website or with the chore of revamping your current website?

Backlinks

You can still have links on it and to it. You just have to be more discriminating about the links to your site and from your site. Have you heard about the Disavow Tool? This is a new tool that Google offers web publishers so that they can improve their website's quality.

When Google cracked down on poor quality links, a lot of people were caught with the results of backlinks that they bought or gathered from link networks that were less than reputable. Buying links is against the Google rules but Google reached out to help people who might be caught with links they wish they did not have because these links have caused them to drop from the top of Google.

Google provides the Disavow Tool that lets a web owner report links that they do not want counted on their sites. The effort to have links from another site to your site can be a challenge. Bad link sources may not want to or they may not have the time or resources to remove the thousands of links they have provided over the years. If you disavow the links before your site is penalized for using them, you can save yourself a lot of grief.

If you are looking over your site to streamline it for future success, look at your incoming links to ensure that they are from good sites. If not, you can ask to have them removed by the web owners and if that does not work, you can disavow them.

If you have a lot of links on your blogroll, remove them just in case someone does not like your site and decides to disavow your site. If a site gets a lot of disavow requests, it does not look good for that site and that could cause you problems in the future.

Speaking of bad links in, if you run a site that allows comments, check into making your comments "no follow" because this will keep shabby links from being posted by people who are just looking for link juice. If you have been allowing people to post just to get their links out there for the world to see, the quality of participation might be low. This will decrease your site's value. Clean up those discussion posts and keep them relevant and clean.

Articles

Go for quality. You don't have to write Pulitzer Prize winning prose. Don't toss out all the keyword SEO information that you have in your head. There are valid reasons for using keywords. Properly used, they do let people know immediately what your site is about.

You don't have to measure the number of words and keywords in an article. It is just a good principle of writing to tell people upfront what the article is about. Use your keyword in the title and in the first paragraph. A rule of thumb is a keyword no more than once every 100 words.

Write with your reader in mind. Really think about what the reader wants. Be personal and open to your readers. Don't follow rigid rules about how long the article should be. Make it valuable. Check your facts. Just because you read it online in someone's blog does not make it a fact.

Be careful when you see ads for new ways to beat the system and rise to page one on Google. You can bet that Google will soon see any signs of news ways to get around the changes and once again have flimsy sites rise to the top and pull the plug on that method too.

Flimsy sites are those that offer nothing new and interesting. It is the nature of some sites that there is not a great deal of information available because you are offering a service such as, for instance, computer repair.

You can provide a lot of information but people coming to your site don't necessarily want to read all about what might be wrong with their computer or how to fix it themselves. They want to know if you can fix it and how long it will take and how much it will cost.

Your site might not have a lot of content but it is a real site offering a real service and it can be optimized for your specific business and location so that if someone searches for Joe's computer repair in Lower Baddeck they will be able to find it because if it is properly SEOed, you will have that information included in the keywords on the site. You don't need to be at the top of the search engines for computer repairs anywhere on the planet. You just need to be found by someone in Lower Baddeck looking for a computer repair person.

Optimizing your website for successful search engine results is all about providing quality. You are not limited to writing. More and more, video is becoming the way to appeal to people. You can add video to your site and have the written version there as well as the video. This appeals to those who like to read and to those who like the visual aspect.

Organize your site so that it easy for people to find things. Even if you have great articles and content, if there is no way for people to find their way from one article or post to the next one, they will become frustrated and leave, never to return.

Post to your site consistently. If you have a blog and only blog one in a while with no consistent pattern, you will have a hard time getting people to return. If you have evergreen content rather than a blog, check it from time to time to make sure all links are working and that the information is still relevant.

Conclusion

This has been a journey through how the World Wide Web works and why search engines are so powerful. Specifically this has been an explanation of why Google is so powerful.

It would be great if there was a way to outline the steps to take that would put your website at the top of the search engines. For the past 10 to 12 years, there have been guides to making your website reach the number one spot and for many people, these methods did work for a little while.

The online world is a very fast-paced environment. People are in a rush to find what they want to find and people are in a rush to get their pages online and in front of interested eyes. The faster that the demand for information grew, the more urgently web publishers sought shortcuts to meeting these demands.

Software was developed to do everything from spin articles to assess your keywords to scrape content to create and post your blogs. Outsourcing became an essential part of doing online business.

The whole framework was in place and a new service industry grew up and while this way of doing business seemed to be permanently in place, this is a very volatile industry. Successful entrepreneurs are those who can focus on a clear goal and find ethical and durable ways to create their online presence.

The rules for SEO are much simpler but this does not mean that the work is much easier. You have to work a little harder to provide the kind of quality that Google demands.

Quick SEO Guidelines

1. Write interesting articles and blogs that make you look real and knowledgeable.
2. Use keywords sparingly but use them.
3. Clean up your backlinks so your site does not suffer from being disavowed.
4. Check the links left on your site to make sure that they are not the cause of poor quality comments.

Amanda's Other Books

Economic Crisis: World Food System - The Battle against Poverty, Pollution and Corruption

Flood Your Websites and Blogs with Free Traffic: Quickly Learn How to Send Visitors to Your Web Sites the Organic Way

Quickly Dominate Social Media Marketing: The Ultimate Guide Top Tips to Pinterest, Google+, Facebook, Twitter, Instagram, LinkedIn and YouTube Viral Marketing

Anti-Aging Guide Top Tips: Inspiration and Helpful Advice to Help You Feel Gorgeous and Look Younger

Home Quick Makeovers Top Tips: Learn How to Design, Decorate and Furnish Your Ideal Home

SEO: Search Engine Optimization

SEO: Search Engine Optimization